Sky and Wind and Star and Poem

PINSON HALL

YOON DONGJU MEMORIAL COMMITTEE

SKY AND WIND AND STAR AND POEM:
BY YOON DONGJU

TRANSLATED BY Suh Hong Won
PLANNED AND EDITED BY Kim Sung Yeun, Jeong Myeong Kyo, Cho Kang Sok
DESIGN BY Workroom Press
PHOTOGRAPHY BY Kim Kyoungtae
PRODUCED BY Yonsei University Press

Yoon Dongju Memorial Museum, Yonsei University,
50 Yonsei-ro Seodaemun-gu,
Seoul, 03722, Republic of Korea
info.museum.dongju@yonsei.ac.kr

ISBN 978-89-6850-382-5 (03810)
₩10,000

Pinson Hall © Kim Kyoungtae

Note

The translation is based on *Sky and Wind and Star and Poem*, edited with notes by Chong Hyon-jong, et al. Seoul: Yonsei University Press, 2012.

Manuscripts:
Yoon Dongju's *Sky and Wind and Star and Poem*, written in the poet's hand, 1941.
Yoon Dongju's Prose, written in the poet's hand, c.1938–1940.

This book is in two sections. The front section (by western standards) contains a translation of the 1941 manuscript of Yoon Dongju's poems, together with 3 pieces of his prose. Beginning from the opposite end is a facsimile of the original manuscripts of the poetry and prose, written in the poet's hand, which reads from right to left.

CONTENTS

PROSE

PREFACE

'Yoon Dongju of Yon-Hui College.'

This was how Yoon Dongju left his name for the last time as a poet, in a newspaper. Yoon Dongju was born in Bukgando on December 30, 1917, in a village called Myeongdong, and died in February 16, 1945, in Fukuoka Prison, Japan, at a young age of 27. He could not see the day of Korea's liberation, which was only half a year away. In 1938, he entered Yon-Hui College (later Yonsei University), then a bulwark against colonial Japan's systematic efforts to destroy Korea's language, history and culture. Yon-Hui College broadened Yoon Dongju's literary horizons, and he wrote some of his best-known poetry, here. Were it not for the professors and friends at Yon-Hui College, our encounter with poet Yoon Dongju might not have been so profound.

Yonsei has not forgotten its poet and has embraced him as one of its own. Yonsei alumni were actively involved in the publication of the 1948 and 1955 volumes of Yoon Dongju's poetry. And in 1968, students, alumni and family gathered in the copse in front of Pinson Hall, the dormitory where Yoon Dongju had spent his college years, to erect Yoon Dongju Poetry Stone in his name. In 2018, the copse in turn was turned into the Yoon Dongju Memorial Grove, and Pinson Hall will be newly opened as Yoon Dongju Memorial Hall. It will be a *larchiveum* (library + archive + museum), a repository of the spirit and culture of youth, where the literary heritage of the poet will be kept alive.

Student-poet Yoon Dongju had planned to publish a collection of poems for charity, to commemorate his graduation in 1941. Colonial Japan's restrictions on the use of the Korean language became prohibitive, however, and the poet had to abort the publication upon the advice of his professor, leaving only three copies of the manuscript written in his own hand. After Yoon Dongju's death, his family and friends had painstakingly gathered his manuscripts and materials relating to him, and in 2013 donated the entire collection to his alma mater. Among the collection, was the only extant copy of the manuscript of the 1941 commemorative collection, guarded through the darkest of times by the poet's friend Jeong Byeonguk. The precious manuscript returned home to Pinson Hall, the dormitory where Yoon Dongju had spent his college life.

To celebrate the opening of Yoon Dongju Memorial Hall, Yonsei University has published the aborted volume of 1941. It took eighty years to fulfill the poet's dream, as he had planned it. All nineteen poems selected by the poet for the charity collection of 1941 have been included, along with three of the poet's prose that contain glimpses of his life and thoughts while at Yon-Hui College. We hope this collection will inspire all readers, whether here at Yonsei University or abroad, where they are about to venture into a new path.

President, Yonsei University

INTRODUCTION

Publishing the Aborted Volume of Poetry: The Story Behind the Volume and Its Significance

We are here setting forth a volume of poetry, of a collection of poems that Yoon Dongju had planned (but aborted) for his graduation from Yon-Hui College, together with three of the prose pieces that he wrote while at Yon-Hui. In essence, this volume is a belated fulfillment of Yoon Dongju's dream, eighty years after its intended publication in 1941. What is the significance of this collection of poems? Why was the poet forced to abort its publication? Why is it meaningful that it was finally published this day? To answer these questions, we must look deep and long into the story of this collection.

Yoon Dongju entered Yon-Hui College on April 9, 1938, and graduated on December 27, 1941. In these four academic years, his "thoughts ripen[ed] of themselves, like apples." His life as a seeker of truth, honed since childhood, came to full maturity at Yon-Hui. Above all, he did not blindly accept what he was taught but tried to reaffirm them one by one in his life. He agonized over the fact that he was not permitted the martyrdom of Jesus Christ ("The Cross") and, so that "no spot of shame / be upon [him]," he "was troubled even by / a slight wind that grew on a leaf" ("Prelude"). Since his encounter with his friends and professors at Yon-Hui College, his conscientious approach to life was transformed into energetic intellectual activities. He published the literary magazine *Munwu* (A Literary Friend) with his cousin Song Monggyu (who had been with him since childhood) and friend Kang Cheojung, and read his poems aloud to Jeong Byeonguk and other friends, listening attentively to their opinions. He wrote forty-one poems (five of them children's verses) and three prose pieces at Yon-Hui College, out of a hundred and nineteen poems and four prose pieces written by him throughout his life, which we have uncovered to this date. If we consider that the majority of the poems written before he entered college are classified as 'children's verse' or 'exercises,' we can tell that his creative years were densely concentrated around the time he attended Yon-Hui College. Song Woohye, author of *Critical Essays on Yoon Dongju*, therefore says of the years he spent at Yon-Hui College that they "can be defined as 'the most fruitful times, the freest times' of his life."

Yoon Dongju planned to publish a volume of poetry under the title *Sky and Wind and Star and Poem*, having selected eighteen of the poems he had written in this period, with the poem "Prelude" attached to the front. It was a type of graduation work. His professor Lee Yangha, however, feared Japanese censorship and advised Yoon Dongju to postpone its publication. He took the professor's advice but instead made three manuscript copies, written in his own hand, of the aborted volume and gave one copy to Professor Lee Yangha, another to Jeong Byeonguk, and kept the last for himself. According to Jeong, the anger expressed in the poem "Liver," which Yoon Dongju wrote immediately afterwards (November 20, 1941), is probably over the aborted publication. And in January 24, 1942, he wrote

"Repentance" probably to atone for his acceptance of a Japanese name, which was unavoidable if he wanted to go abroad and enter a Japanese college. In the last lines of "Liver," he wrote:

> Prometheus, poor Prometheus,
> Prometheus who, for the crime of stealing fire,
> is wearing a millstone and is endlessly sinking.

Lamenting his plight of having to keep his head under Japanese surveillance, but nevertheless strengthening his resolve that he must not stop dreaming, he depicts himself as a "Prometheus who … is wearing a millstone and is endlessly sinking."

In the spring of 1942, he crossed the sea to Japan. At first, he entered Rikkyo University in Tokyo, but in the fall he moved to Kyoto to enter Doshisha University. On July 14, 1943, four days after the arrest of Song Monggyu, he was arrested and jailed at Shimogamo Police Station under the suspicion of plotting Korean independence. And on March 31, 1944, he was sentenced to "two years in prison" and was locked up in Fukuoka Prison. According to Song Monggyu's testimony, he was "injected with an unknown substance every day" and died the following year, on February 16, 1945. His body was turned over to his father and uncle and, after it was cremated, the ashes returned home to Longjing (Jilin, China) and were buried on March 6 in Dongsan Church Cemetery. The same year, "around Dano Festival [fifth day of the fifth lunar month], his family erected a gravestone with the inscription 'Grave of Poet Yoon Dongju'."

Meanwhile, Jeong Byeonguk, who had received a copy of the manuscript written in Yoon Dongju's hand, was abruptly conscripted to the Japanese colonial army in 1943, while still a student. Having already heard of Yoon's arrest, he handed the manuscript to his mother and begged her to keep it safe. Jeong's mother wrapped the bundle of poetry "in layers of silk cloth" and took it to the family home in Gwangyang, Jeollanamdo, where she dug a large hole in the ground, hidden under the wooden floor of the house, and "having spread the straw at the bottom of the hole, placed a huge jar in it," and then hid the manuscript in the jar, along with other precious belongings. It was preserved with such care that, after Korean independence and the return of Jeong Byeonguk, the manuscript Yoon Dongju had placed in his care was recovered in almost pristine form. This became the only surviving manuscript of the volume of poems, left behind by the poet who was no longer with us.

A golden opportunity for Yoon Dongju's manuscript, which was preserved with such care, arose in February 1947. His friend Kang Cheojung introduced "A Poem Easily Written," written while Yoon Dongju was studying in Japan, in *Kyunghyang Shinmun*. This became an astonishing and extraordinary event because "editor of *Kyunghyang Shinmun* and one of the foremost poets of the time Jeong Jiyong had attached an introductory note" to the poem. "Under the conditions then, it was perhaps the best way for an unknown poet to appear before the world."

Yoon Dongju's family erected for him a gravestone with the inscription "Grave of Poet Yoon Dongju", but he had never formally 'stepped on' to the literary world. "Stepping on" to the literary world is a custom born of peculiar circumstances in Korea, but in reality, it has acted as a strong barrier to aspiring writers and even today continues unwaning in its power. What Yoon Dongju's family did was simply a private means of fulfilling his aspirations. But Jeong Jiyong's 'introduction' gave an official stamp of approval to the family's action.

How was this possible? Jeong Jiyong says in his introduction of Yoon Dongju:

> On February 26 [note: correct date is 16] of the year of Japan's surrender, at the height of atrocities, Japan assassinated a young poet in bloom, under the charge of *futei senjin* (malcontent Korean), and was itself destroyed. Poet Yoon Dongju's remains are buried in Yongjung (Korean pronunciation of Longjing), and ten or so of his sorrowful poems are with me. They will be serially presented, as newspaper space permits, and for this I am proud, more so than Mr. Yoon himself will be.

Jeong Jiyong's introduction contains far too much emotion for an introduction of an unknown poet. A desire to find compensation for Japan's crimes, wholly through Yoon Dongju's poems, seems fervidly at work here.

In fact, the question of the *raison d'être* of Korean literature after Liberation is profoundly involved. Let us begin with the fact that, by the 1940s, Korea had undergone thirty years of Japanese colonialism. Furthermore, the Korean people in the peninsula had not even the slightest notion that Japan would be defeated. Thus, Ham Seokheon said of the Liberation that it "came like a thief." Meanwhile, having provoked the War, Japan needed to deploy vast resources and was tightening its reins on its colonies. The deployment of resources was not limited to the material but also required spiritual unity, or rather uniformity. In this vein, use of the Korean language in the Korean peninsula was prohibited, and in its place, Japanese was to be used in all places. These injunctions trapped the literati of the peninsula into a double, triple layer of confinement. They were not only to cooperate with Japan's political propaganda but were also to write literary works only in Japanese.

But suddenly Japan was defeated in the Second World War and surrendered to the allied forces in 1945. Korea gained independence, and its leaders were tasked with the construction of the newly free state. Japan was no longer the 'homeland' of Korea, and neither was it clearly a model of a modern state, to be imitated by the Koreans. Furthermore, from the moment of surrender, the Japanese language lost its status as a lingua franca among Japan's former colonies. With independence, just as the 'nation' was handed to Koreans in the raw, so were the Korean letters, Hangul, 'returned' to Korean literary circles as the true but difficult medium of expression. But the writers and critics of this liberated space were not quite assured whether they were qualified or able to take on the new world that lay before them. In the long years of colonization, they had progressed too far into subservience to and integration with Japan. Even under such bleak conditions, was it possible that someone could have been resisting? Could they not have been preparing for an independent state, each in their own way?

Koreans were painfully in need of evidence to convince themselves that they were able and qualified to bear the weight of the liberated nation. It was owning to such history that three poets who had "stepped on" to the literary scene in the early 1940s, but had lost their opportunity to publish their poetry because of Japanese attempts to systematically eradicate the Korean language, refusing in their minds to write in Japanese and honing their skills in the Korean language, as they locked themselves up in small rooms to write Korean poetry, were able to reappear spectacularly in the post-independence literary world, under the collective name of the "Blue Deer School." It could be said that the same logic applied to Yoon Dongju, who was a victim of colonial violence. He was arrested for plotting Korean liberation and died in prison, having undergone suspicious medical treatment that suggested 'human trial.' And he had left something behind—none other than poetry and prose written in Korean. These writings were clear evidence that something meaningful had emerged from Yoon Dongju's sacrifice.

Foremost critic Paek Chul thus tells us that "in response to the words 'dark ages' to denote the five years including and after 1941 … [s]ome young writer [expressed] dissatisfaction, explaining that these years could not be called such because of the presence of poet Yoon Dongju," to which the critic offered, "could we not rather call this age the age of *resistance*?" Jeong Byeonguk similarly questions, "Is *resistance* literature that fights to the death against tyranny and oppression — to safeguard the spirit of defiance while receiving support merely from a frail body, rather to safeguard freedom that is the first and the last right and property of a human being — only to be a prerogative of European intellectuals?" He adds confidently that "the poetic spirit of Yoon Dongju, who 'was troubled even by / a slight wind that grew on a leaf, … [sang] of stars' that safeguarded the nation and freedom through the night, against the fierce 'rustl[ing] … wind' of tyranny and oppression." Both critics may have expressed common hopes under common circumstances.

The introductory note in *Kyunghyang Shinmun* by Jeong Jiyong, great poet and teacher of the times, and the "Prelude" attached to the front of the first published collection in 1948 officially confirmed these hopes. Through the efforts of friends and family, carefully prepared memorial events gave further mandate to such hopes and spread the message of hope to ordinary readers.

The introduction of poet Yoon Dongju is recorded as the most notable event in the history of Korean literature. The circumstantial conditions that contributed to the felicitous 'birth' of the poet, however, did not by any means certify his literary stature. The formal beauty and perfection of the poems he left behind, and the expressions of feelings that come deeply from inside, resonated in the hearts of his readers and raised the estimation among the critics, resulting in the explosive growth of his readership in Korea. Of Yoon Dongju's poems, Jeong Jiyong wrote: "What though I did not know the poet Yoon Dongju? Is it not enough that Yoon Dongju's poetry is truly 'poetry'? [...] It is not difficult the know a 'poet' by his 'poetry'." Of Yoon Dongju as a poet, he added that the poet was "a flower in the last day of the wintry year, a carp underneath the layer of ice." Kim Sambul, Yoon Dongju's classmate at Yon-Hui College, "presented" an "academic study of the greatness of Yoon Dongju's poetry" on the second anniversary of the poet's death, February 16, 1947. Kim's emphasis on the literary value of Yoon Dongju's poetic world was yet another effort at establishing Yoon Dongju among the celestial circle of poets.

Yoon Dongju's status in Korean literature and the significance of his life both spring from the well of his poetry. That is why, whenever we talk or think about Yoon Dongju, we do so through his poems. Each poem glitters with warm, suggestive mouthfuls from the vast fount that swells with the details of the poet's life, from his humble and earnest search for purity in life to his critical awareness of and resistance to the tragic conditions of Korea under the violence of colonial Japan, and to its final and fated culmination in martyrdom. The reader, taking a sip and rolling it on the tip of her tongue, will experience a full life sprouting from a fragment of language and filling the whole mouth with its savory essences.

Now we can understand better the reason behind the publication of this volume of poetry. By restoring the collection of poems to its originally planned organization, we can get a glimpse of Yoon Dongju's literary flower bed. Through this the reader can witness the entire process of the birth of Yoon Dongju's poetry. Next, by fulfilling the poet's aborted dream, this collection will serve as a space where we may commemorate and appease the unfortunate poet's soul. Here, the reader will be able to reflect on the profound significance of connecting one's life with another person's fate. Lastly, above all, this volume of poetry will serve as an opportunity to embark on an adventure into another life. The possibility of facing dangerous sedition, even when one has not attempted it, is an inevitability that literature must gladly endure in its search for entire truths. In recompense for accepting such dangers, literature draws nearer to the fundamental nature of humanity and the inscrutable truths of life that are unreachable through any other human endeavor. Moreover, it will preserve in eternal and irreducible memory the sense of absolute freedom, experienced in the execution of the literary enterprise.

Indeed, neither blatant themes of resistance nor criticism of real life can be clearly detected while reading the poems of Yoon Dongju. Nevertheless, if the reader strongly experiences the unjust violence of life and the opposing motions of blameless resistance, it is because his poetry is connected to the fundamental ontology of literature that we have mentioned just moments ago. In this respect, we can say that his poetry offers a fundamental example for all literary projection. This collection of poems may be considered the root form of such a model. I am confident that this collection will act as a guide, cool as a splash of cold water, to the reader who wishes to experience the vivid emotions of reading Yoon Dongju's poetry and prose.

Jeong Myeong Kyo
Department of Korean Language and Literature,
Yonsei University

Window of Pinson Hall © Kim Kyoungtae

Prelude

Till my dying day, let no spot of shame
be upon me, as I look to heaven;
I was troubled even by
a slight wind that grew on a leaf.
I will love all that is dying
with a heart that sings of stars,
and walk the path that
is given me.

Even tonight a star is rustled by the wind.

Self-portrait

Around the mountain by the fields, a solitary well I seek alone and steadily look into it.

In the well the moon is bright and the cloud is adrift and the sky is wide and the blue wind is blowing and autumn is there.

And a man is there.
For some reason, I find myself hating the man and turn away.

On the way back, I feel a pity for the man. I return and look in, and the man is there as I left him.

Again, I find myself hating the man and turn away.
On the way back, I feel a longing for the man.

In the well, the moon is bright and the cloud is adrift and the sky is wide and the blue wind is blowing and autumn is there and the man is there like a memory.

The Youth

Here and there sad autumn is falling, falling like maple leaves. Spring has been provided for, everywhere where the leaves have fallen, and the sky is spread wide on the branches. As he looks steadily at the sky, his eyebrows are dyed blue. He brushes his warm cheeks with his two hands and looks, and blue paint has rubbed off on his palms. He looks at his hands again. In the lines of his palms a clear river flows, a clear river flows, and in the river a face sad as love—the face of beautiful Suni glimmers. The youth closes his eyes in bliss. Even so the clear river flows, and even so the face sad as love—the face of beautiful Suni glimmers.

Snow Falls on the Map

In the morning Suni is leaving, snow falls with unspoken heaviness and blankets, as if in sorrow, the map outside the window, vanishing into the distance.

I look around the room, but no one is there. Walls and ceiling are white. Is snow falling inside the room, even? Are you truly to go so fleetingly like forgotten history? I know not where you are going; no street, no town, no roofed house to send a letter, to tell you what I meant to say before you left—are you to remain only in my thoughts? I cannot follow your little footprints, covered with snow falling upon snow. When snow melts, flowers will bloom along the path of the remaining footprints, and as I weave myself among flowers in search of the footprints, snow will fall all the year long on my white thoughts.

The Night of My Return

As if to return from the world, I now return to my narrow room and turn off the light. To leave the light on is a thing too tiring. It being an extension of day—

Time to open the window and let in the air for a change, but a long steady look outside shows a dark as dark as the room, dark like the world, and the path I took back to my room under the rain remains wet in the rain.

Unable to wash away the day's anger I close my eyes, and a sound flows in my mind, and now my thoughts ripen of themselves, like apples.

Hospital

Hiding her face in the shadow of a peach tree, a young woman lies in the backyard of a hospital, white legs under white clothes, bathing under the sun. Up till the waning sun no one comes to visit this woman, who they say has an ailing heart. Not even a butterfly. Not even a breeze on the branches of the peach tree that is not even sorrowful.

Having long suffered an ailment I have no knowledge of, I have for the first time sought out this place. But my old doctor does not comprehend the sickness of the youth. He says I have no sickness. This exceeding trial, this exceeding fatigue, I must not rage.

The woman gets up, tidies her clothes, plucks a marigold from a flower bed, sticks it on her chest and disappears into her hospital room. Hoping for the swift recovery of the woman's health—no mine, too—I try lying down on the spot where she lay.

A New Path

Across the stream into the woods
over the hill into the village

Yesterday and today
my path a new path

Dandelion blooms and magpie flies
maiden passes and wind arises

My path always a new path
today ... and tomorrow ...

Across the stream into the woods
over the hill into the village

Street without Signboards

No one at the platform
when I got off the bus

All are but visitors
people looking only like visitors

No signboards on shops
no worries finding the way

No blazing letters
in red
or blue

Each corner
lighted by
kind, worn-out gaslights

Touch their sleeves and
gentle folk, all
gentle folk, all

Spring, summer, autumn, winter,
going around by turn

Morning, in the Beginning

On a morning not spring
not summer, autumn, winter,
not that kind of morning

A red flower blossomed
though sunlight was blue

The night before
the night before
everything was provided for

Love, along with the snake
poison, along with the young flower

Morning, in the Beginning, Again

Covered all white with snow
telegraph poles buzz and buzz
Words of God to my ear.

What could the revelation be.

Early
when spring arrives
I will sin
eyes
clear

When Eve is done with the pains of labor

Hiding my privates with a fig leaf

I will perspire from my forehead.

Till Dawn Arrives

For all who are dying
dress them in black.

For all who are living
dress them in white.

And put them to sleep
neatly on one bed.

And when they all cry
feed them on the breast.

Now when dawn arrives
trumpets will sound from afar.

Time of Fear

What! Who is it that calls on me?

In the shadow where parched leaves are sprouting green,
here I remain still breathing.

I who have never waved a hand
I who have no heaven to wave to

Where is the heaven where I may trust my body
that it calls on me?

When work is done on the morn of my death
the parched leaf not even sorrowful will fall....

Do not call on me.

The Cross

It was a sunlight chasing me, but
now it hangs on a cross
on the top of a chapel.

How does it climb atop,
the spire being so high?

No church bells are ringing, but
I'll hang around whistling, and

If, as if
to the man in agony,
happy Jesus Christ,
the cross is permitted me

Neck long stretched out
under the darkening sky
I will quietly shed
blood blooming like a flower.

The Wind Blows

From whence does the wind blow
and whither is it blowing?

The wind blows, but
there is no reason for my agony

Is there no reason for my agony?

I have never loved even one woman
neither have I mourned over the times

The wind keeps on blowing, but
my feet stand on a rock

The river keeps on flowing, but
my feet stand on a hill

A Sorrowful Race

White towel wraps around their black head, and
white rubber shoes hang on their rough feet.

White top and dress hide their sorrowful body, and
white band wraps tight around their slender waist.

Go with Eyes Shut

You children who adore the sun
you children who love the stars

Night has darkened
go with eyes shut.

As you go scatter
the seeds that you have.

If a stone catches your toes
open your shut eyes wide.

The Other Hometown

The night I returned to my hometown
a skeleton followed and lay down in my room.

The dark room leads to the universe, and
from the sky a wind blows like a sound.

I look at the skeleton
prettily weathering in the dark
shedding tears; is it me that is crying, or
is it the skeleton that is crying, or
is it the beautiful soul that is crying?

The loyal dog
keeps vigil and barks at the dark.

The dog that barks at the dark
is most likely chasing after me.

Let us go let us go
let us go like a man being chased.
Steal away from the skeleton and
let us go to the beautiful, other hometown.

The Path

I had lost it.
Not knowing what I'd lost or where,
both hands searching my pockets
I go out to the path.

Stone upon stone upon stone endless
the path leads along the stone wall.

The wall's iron gates are firmly closed
casting a long shadow on the path

And the path leads from morning to evening
from evening to morning.

Finding my way with my hands on the wall, in tears,
I look up, and the sky is shamefully blue.

I walk this path that is without even a blade of grass
because I remain on the other side of the wall

And I live only because
I seek what I have lost.

One Night, Counting the Stars

The sky when the season passes
is filled to the full with the fall.

I could almost count, free of care,
all the stars in the folds of this fall.

If I cannot complete the counting of stars
that are etched one and two in my heart,
it is that morn arrives too hastily,
that tomorrow night is yet to come, and
that my youth is not yet done.

A star and remembrance
A star and love
A star and loneliness
A star and longing
A star and poem
A star and mother, mother.

Mother, for each star I sing the syllables of beautiful words.
Names of children who sat next to me in school,
names of foreign girls like 'Pae,' 'Kyeong,' 'Ok';
names of girls already become mothers;
names of poor neighbors; pigeon, puppy, rabbit, donkey, deer;
names of poets like 'Francis Jammes,' 'Reiner Maria Rilke.'

These are too distant.
Distant as the shimmering stars.

Mother,
and, you are distant in Bukkando.

For whatever longing
on a hill showered with the rays of numerous stars,
I spelled out my name on the earth
and covered it over with soil.

Perhaps, even, the cricket cries all night
sadly ashamed of its own name.

But when winter passes and spring comes to my star,
just as green grass grows on burial mounds,
so will it grow rich and proud
on the hill where my name is buried.

PROSE

Shoot at the Moon

The hustle and bustle around me have quieted down, and I can hear clearly the ticking of the clock. Night must have deepened quite. I push my books to the edge of the desk, tidy the bed and put on my sleeping clothes. With a click of the switch I turn off the lamp and lie down on the bed by the window. Till then I had not sensed that the night outside was splendidly lit by the moon. Had I enjoyed too much the benefit of the clear lamp?

Rather than turning into a beautiful picture when suffused in moonlight, my humble room becomes a sorrowful wharf. The bars of the window linger on my forehead, moving on to the bridge of my nose, my lips, even on to the back of my hand held close to my chest, and tickles my mind. The room becomes terrible with the breathing of the person lying in the next bed. Heart beating wildly like a child, I lift up my eyes and look out the window, and the autumn sky is clear as expected, and the dense pine forest is a landscape, black ink on white. Moonlight pours down on the pine branches and almost, as if it were the wind, makes a rustling sound. But all I hear are the sounds of the clock, the breathing, and the crickets singing. The bustling dormitory is now more silent than a Buddhist temple.

I am deeply plunged into thought. Well, thoughts of a beautiful portrait bringing up contemplations of a lovely young girl would have been good, or thoughts of my hometown where I have left so many wistful memories would also have been good, but there is something more serious that defies easy expression,

The more I think of the letter sent by my friend H from across the sea, the more subtly complex appear the emotions that pass between one person and another. For certain, autumn must have arrived inevitably upon the sentimental man.

Isn't the letter a bit too much! Here is a piece of it:

"Dear boy! I cry as I write this letter. This night, too, the moon rises and wind blows, and as I am a human being I know the smell of the soil named autumn. The tears of affection, the tears of affection of one who was a student artist will be the last that are shed when the night is done."

Also, in the last part is this phrase:

"Driving me away forever would be the honest thing for you to do."

I can decipher the nuance of these words. But in truth I have never said a painful word to him, nor have I sent him any piece of writing that could cause him sorrow! In my mind, I can only blame autumn for the sin.

Presumptuous though it may be for a pink-faced student of letters to conclude such a thing, friends are merely beings that bring you agony, and friendship truly is water poured into a precarious vessel. Who is it that can deny this? But as it is said, it is hard to acquire a true friend, and to lose a cherished friend is to feel the pain of cutting out of one's own flesh.

I discover myself in the yard, and I need not rack my brain foolishly on whether I came out through the window or whether by opening the door, or wherefore I had come out. It is enough that I stand quietly hidden before a cosmos flower, shy even at the singing of crickets, sad as the shadow of the statue of Dr. Billings [Billingsley]. I have no sour wish to pass these feelings onto anyone else. My collars are sensitive and frost even to moonlight, and autumn dews are so chilling as to become the sorrowful tears of a man.

My steps carry this body and place it by the pond. In the pond, there is autumn as expected, and there is midnight and trees, and there is the moon. (There is the moon....) That instant I blame autumn and begin to dislike the moon. Searching with my hands I find a stone and throw it at the moon with all my might. Release! The moon has been shattered to pieces. But when the frightened water quiets down, the moon soon returns to life! I suddenly look up to the sky, and there is the hateful moon smirking above my head—

I grasp a straight branch, bind it tight, and string it into a bow. Then, taking a sturdy reed as an arrow, I put on a warrior's heart and shoot at the moon.

Where the Shooting Star Falls

It is night.

The sky is so blue that it has darkened to a dense gray, but the stars are shining all the more clearly. Not only is it dimly dark but it is also shivering cold. In the midst of this weighty air is a young man mocking himself. Let us call him me.

I am conceived in this darkness, grown in this darkness and, it seems, still surviving in this darkness. Now, not knowing whither I should go, I flounder. Indeed I am pale, as if I were the focus of the century. On brief inspection, it may appear as if I have nothing properly to support my two feet, nor for that matter anything to press down hard on my head, but under the surface it is not what it seems. I am not free at all. I am nothing more than a gnat, existing but non-existent, floating in air. Were it the levity of the gnat, it would be a relief, but it is not.

There appears to be another, different focus of brightness lurking at a spot symmetrically opposite to this point. Were I to grab it suddenly I may be able to catch it.

But I may be too clumsy, or my mind is clearly not at all ready or have not planned for it, to be able to grasp firmly. Come to think of it, to invite an extraordinary guest called happiness, one would have to pay with yet another string of excuses.

That this night is a mere veil of terror to me, as in the days of childhood, has become already a legend gone by. To be told, however, that this night is a cauldron of pleasure is, to my mind, a rock I cannot yet digest. It is enough that the night is an opponent worthy of my challenge.

If this were to remain only in the vivid realm of thought, it were indeed a shame. That thatch-roofed houses, dozing in the dark and clustered together in neat rows, can become elegant lines in a beautiful poem is a story of a past generation. Today, they are merely a backdrop for unspeakable tragedy.

Now, say that a cock, fluttering his wings and letting out a piercing cry, chases away the night and, driving out the dark, ushers in a new guest called dawn from the luminous east. We should not, however, welcome it so lightly. Look, even if dawn came, this village is as gloomy as before, and I am as gloomy as before, and thus you and I are beings that cannot but waver in the crossroads.

There is a tree.

He is and old neighbor and friend. This does not mean that he and I have a common nature or background or life. It can be, so to speak, nothing more than an example of a miraculous acquaintance, of a love that can penetrate even between two extremes.

At first, I considered him trivial, quite an unfortunate being. When I stood before him I felt saddened, and my eyes were often blinded by pity. But today, as I think back, it appears there can never again be a living thing happier than the tree. Even in a rock uncomparable in hardness, they say there is nourishment, however inadequate; therefore where is that place where one cannot take root, and where is that place where one cannot take comfort in living? When he is wet a soft winds blows to dry him, and when he feels listless a bird comes and sings for him for a while before it flies away, and when he is dried and shriveled a shower of rain quenches his thirst, and when it is night he can converse intimately with countless stars. Moreover, the tree is not confronted with the cumbersome task of deciding on a course of action. He guards the place that gave him birth, whether by the hands of people or by chance, drinks in inexhaustible nourishment and takes in the sparkling sunlight, leading his own life with ease. Is he not happy above all else that he need only look up to the sky and stretch out his branches?

As I worry over a problem I cannot solve, the tree's mind seems to infect my mind, little by little. And though I agonize that I cannot boast of a boast that I can act on, as a friend says in his oration that he himself cannot be trusted, should I then ask my directions to the intelligent tree?

Where should I go, where is east, where west, where south, where north, alas? Where the shooting star has fallen must be where I should go. Then, you shooting star! Fall where you must fall.

Flowers Bloom in the Garden

Forsythia, azelea, violet, lilac, dandelion, wild rose, peach blossom, eglantine, sweetbrier, peony, lily, sweet flag, tulip, carnation, impatient, balsam, zinnia, rose moss, dahlia, sunflower, cosmos—the day cosmos drops all of a sudden is not the end of the universe. Here the blue sky deepens and red, yellow leaves dye each branch as colorful as the flowers, until the fall-colored world tumbles down with the sudden end of the crickets' singing. Then, overnight, white snow falls and covers all in a heap, and charcoal glows red the brazier, and around it many a story is told, many a deed done.

My dear readers! Do not assume that the writing of this essay takes place in a particular season. No, you could as well set it to any season—spring, summer, autumn, winter. In truth, it cannot be spring all through the year. But would it be too much self advertising if it were said that, in this garden, my spring is as equally fresh as the youths, through all seasons? Creating a flower bed is not an easy thing but requires hardship and effort.

No doubt, though I put together some words to scratch out this poor piece of writing, I am not very smart. In the past year, a meager few lines have been written, line by line with my body, not with my head. For me, therefore, writing cannot be an act of joy. I wear myself out with the cares of the spring wind, wither at the tedium of green profusion, cry sentimentally over the autumn sky, drowse in roadside contemplation, and with these few lines, along with my garden, my year is done.

Everyone will know the meaning and charm of the expression 'to eat time', whether one has stood before a blackboard or sat beneath it. Eating time is indeed, truly a joyful thing. Rather than to have a class cancelled for the whole day (no doubt one could just as well sneak away and play hooky), if one had not enough time to prepare for class or to do homework, or were feeling bored or drowsy, an hour of class cancellation would truly be nourishing, and, though the professor could not come because he was sick, we taking nourishment would not have the presence of mind to pay our respects to him.

You should not, however, decide so soon that our words are mere verbiage and a waste of time. There is laughter in a blade of green grass and in a bunch of red blossoms. Who can deny that one could examine truth more clearly, acquire more knowledge, gain more effective achievements than wetting the notebook with ink, than wrestling with lines of writing in the throes of worry and anger?

I can spend this precious time quietly slipping away from my friends and strolling all alone in the garden. But how fortunate is it that one can converse with the flowers and the grass! Truly I can face them with a warm heart, and they greet me with laughter. Would it be too sentimental to answer their laughter with tears? Solitariness and silence are indeed truly beautiful things, but to have friends, also, that care for each other is without doubt a fortunate thing. Of the friends that are gathered in the garden, there is A who says that, during the evenings when he was writing a letter home to ask for tuition fees, he could barely write a meager few lines after deliberation followed by deliberation; B who says that his hands are shaking upon the receipt of a document that he should be happy with (so-called monthly pay); C who says that he loses his appetite and forgets sleep for the sake of love; D who promises suicide over an ideological impasse.... I can understand these pitiful feelings of my several friends, as if they were mine. We can greet each other with a generous mind.

I may have agonized over the wind, cloud, sunlight, tree and friendship, such as these more than over outlook on the world or on life, or over some such larger issues. Do these words merely expose my contradictions or make me a lesser being?

The general public says that today's student morals have been corrupted. They say that we do not know how to honor our teachers. They are right. I am simply ashamed. But should you yoke this defect on our suffering shoulders and drive us out to the wilderness? If there is a teacher who knows where we are hurting, if there is a world that warmly caresses our wounds, we will honor the teacher with all the weight of our morals, denied as they are.

When the world is rumbling with the sound of guns year after year, is it going against the times to come together and understand each other in our garden, and have □□ as before, in the midst of extreme quiet?

When spring is gone and summer is gone and autumn [is here], the day the cosmos drops all of a sudden is not the end of the universe. There is the fall-colored world—履霜而堅氷至 "when you step on frost, be ready for hardening ice"—no, we will step on frosted fallen leaves and trust that spring will come from afar.

At the roadside, many things will be achieved.

윤동주의 백석시집 필사본과 소장소서 ©김경태 Yoon Dongju's book collection, including a copy of poetry by Baek Seok written in Yoon's hand ©Kim Kyoungtae

연세대학교에 기증된 윤동주 유품 ©김경태 Possessions of Yoon Dongju donated to Yonsei University ©Kim Kyoungtae

핀슨관(1936) © 연세대학교 박물관
Pinson Hall (1936) © Yonsei University Museum

하늘과 바람과 별과 詩

핀슨관(1928) ©연세대학교 박물관
Pinson Hall (1928) © Yonsei University Museum

하늘과 바람과 별과 詩

산문(散文)

No.

하늘과바람과별과詩

— 童舟 —

鄭炳昱兄 앞에.

尹東柱 呈.

十行 廿字詰

죽는 날까지 하늘을 우러러
한점 부끄럼이 없기를,
잎새에 이는 바람에도
나는 괴로워했다.
별을 노래하는 마음으로
모든 죽어가는 것을 사랑해야지
그리고 나한테 주어진 길을
걸어가야겠다.

오늘밤에도 별이 바람에 스치운다.

1941.11.20.

7

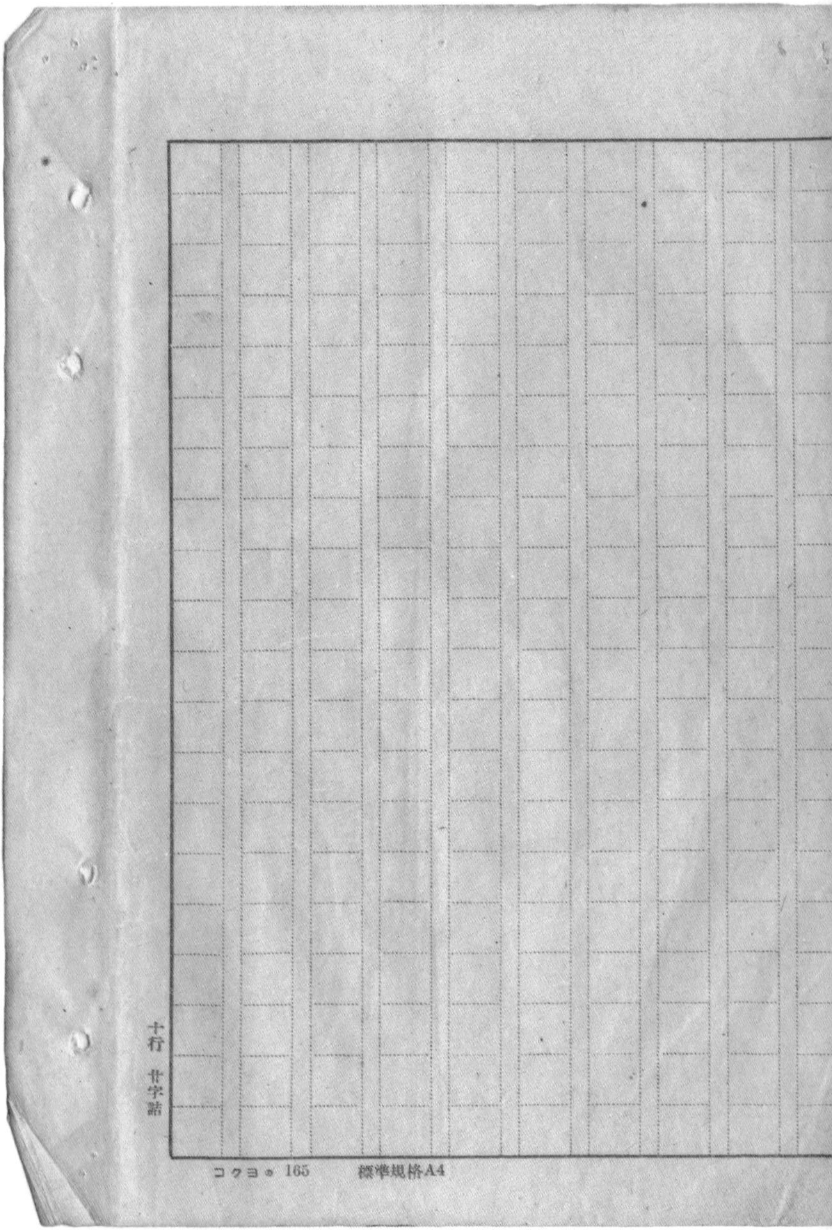

自畵像

산모퉁이를 돌아 논가 외딴 우물을 홀로
찾어가선 가만히 드려다 봅니다.

우물속에는 달이 밝고 구름이 흐르고
하늘이 펼치고 파아란 바람이 불고 가
을이 있습니다.

그라고 한 사나이가 있습니다.
어쩐지 그 사나이가 미워저 돌아갑니다.

돌아가다 생각하니 그 사나이가 가엽서 집니다. 도로가 드려다 보니 사나이는 그대로 있습니다.

다시 그 사나이가 미워저 돌아갑니다.
돌아가다 생각하니 그 사나이가 그리워 집니다.

十行 廿字詰

No.

우물속에는 달이 밝고 구름이 흐르고 하늘이 펼치고 파
아란 바람이 불고 가을이 있고 追憶처
럼 사나이가 있습니다.

一九三九.九.

10

II

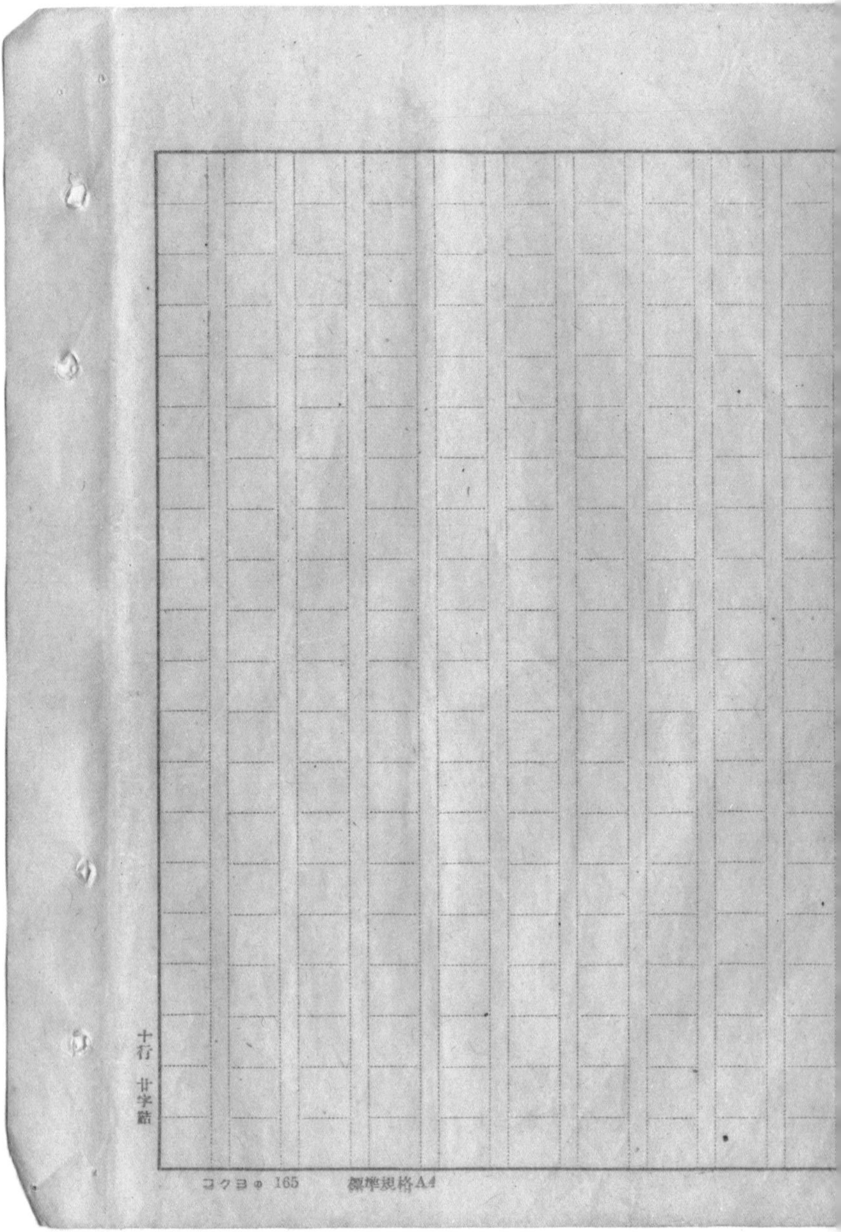
十行 廿字詰

コクヨ ゆ 165 標準規格A4

No.

少年

여기저기서 단풍잎 같은 슬픈 가을이 뚝
뚝 떨어진다. 단풍잎 떨어져 나온 자리
마다 봄을 마련해 놓고 나무가지 우에
하늘이 펼쳐있다. 가만~~히~~이 하늘을 드려다
보려면 눈섭에 파란 물감이 든다. 두손
으로 따뜻한 볼을 쓰서보면 손바닥에도
파란 물감이 묻어난다. 다시 손바닥을 들

드려다 본다. 손금에는 맑은 강물이 흐르고、맑은 강물이 흐르고、강물속에는 사랑처럼 슬픈얼골 — 아름다운 順伊의 얼골이 어린다. 少年은 황홀이 눈을 감어 본다. 그래도 맑은 강물은 흘러 사랑처럼 슬픈얼골 — 아름다운 順伊의 얼골은 어린다.

一九三九.

눈오는 地圖

順伊가 떠난다는 아츰에 말못할 마음으로 함박눈이 나려, 슬픈것처럼 窓밖에 아득히 깔린 地圖우에 덮힌다。

房안을 도라다 보아야 아무도 없다。壁과 天井이 하얗다。房안에까지 눈이 나리는 것일까、정말 너는 잃어버린 歷史처럼 홀홀이 가는것이냐、떠나기前에 일러

들말이 있든것을 편지를 써서도 네가
가는 곳을 몰라 어느거리、 어느마을、 어
느집웅밑、 너는 내 마음속에만 남어 있는
것이냐、 네 쪼고만 빨자욱을 눈이 작고
나려덮혀 따라갈수도 없다。 눈이 녹으
면 남은 발자욱자리마다 꽃이 되리니
꽃사이로 발자욱을 찾어 나서면 一年열
두달 하냥 내마음에는 눈이 나리리라。

一九四一、三、一二、

No.

돌아와 보는 밤

세상으로부터 돌아오듯이 이제 내 좁은 방에 돌아와 불을 끄옵니다. 불을 켜두는 것은 너무나 피로롭은 일이옵니다. 그것은 낮의 延長이옵기에 ——

이제 窓을 열어 空氣를 바꾸어 드려야 할텐데 밖을 가만이 내다보아야 방안

과같이 어두어 꼭 세상같은데 비를 맞
고 오든 길이 그대로 비속에 젖어 있사
옵니다.

하로의 울분을 씻을바 없어 가만히 눈
을 감으면 마음속으로 흐르는 소리, 이
제, 思想이 능금처럼 저절로 익어 가옵
니다.

一九四一、六.

病院

살구나무 그늘로 얼굴을 가리고, 病院 뒷
뜰에 누어, 젊은 女子가 흰옷아래로 하
얀다리를 드려내 놓고 日光浴을 한다.
한나절이 기울도록 가슴을 앓는다는 이
女子를 찾어 오는 이, 나비 한마리도
없다. 슬프지도 않은 살구나무가지에는
바람조차 없다.

나도 모를 아픔을 오래 참다 처음으로 이곳에 찾어왔다. 그러나 나의 늙은 의사는 젊은이의 病을 모른다. 나안테는 病이 없다고 한다. 이 지나친 試鍊, 이 지나친 疲勞, 나는 성내서는 않된다.

女子는 자리에서 일어나 옷깃을 여미고 花壇에서 金盞花 한포기를 따 가슴에 꼽고 病室안으로 살어진다. 나는 그女子

19

十行 廿字詰

No.

의 健康이 ―― 아니 내 健康도 速히 回復되기를 빠라며 그가 누었든 자리에 누어본다。

一九四〇、一二、

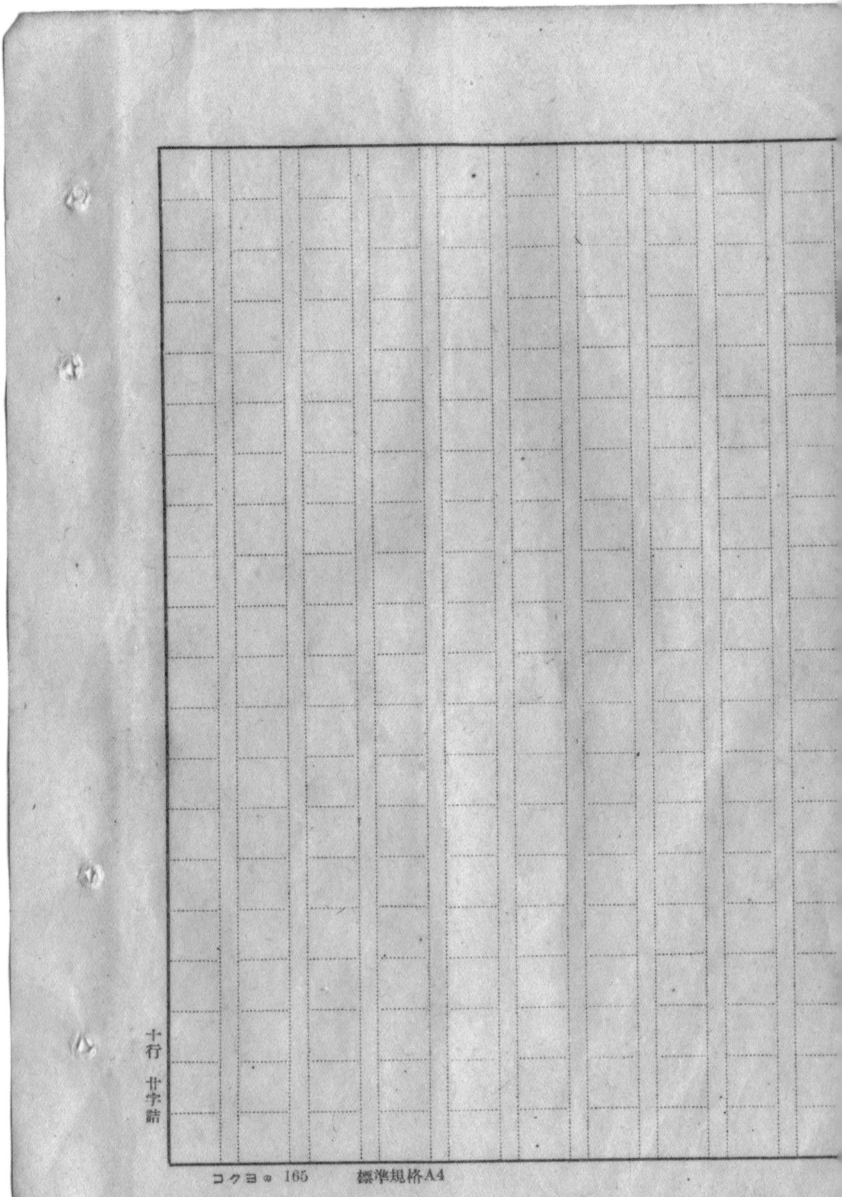
十行 廿字詰
コクヨ 165 標準規格A4

No.

새로운 길

내를 건너서 숲으로

고개를 넘어서 마을로

어제도 가고 오늘도 갈

나의 길 새로운 길

문들레가 피고 가치가 날고

아가씨가 지나고 바람이 일고

나의 길은 언제나 새로운 길
오늘도...... 내일도......

내를 건너서 숲으로
고개를 넘어서 마을로

一九三八. 五. 一〇.

十行 廿字詰

コクヨ 165 標準規格A4

看板없는 거리

停車場 프랕폼에
나렸을 때 아무도 없어,

다들 손님들뿐,
손님 같은 사람들뿐,

집집마다 看板이 없어

집 찾을 근심이 없어

빨가케
파라케
불붙는 文字도 없이

모퉁이마다
慈愛로운 헌 瓦斯燈에
불을 혀놓고,

손목을 잡으면
다들, 어진 사람들
다들, 어진 사람들

No.

봄, 여름, 가을, 겨울,

순서로 돌아 들고,

一九四一.

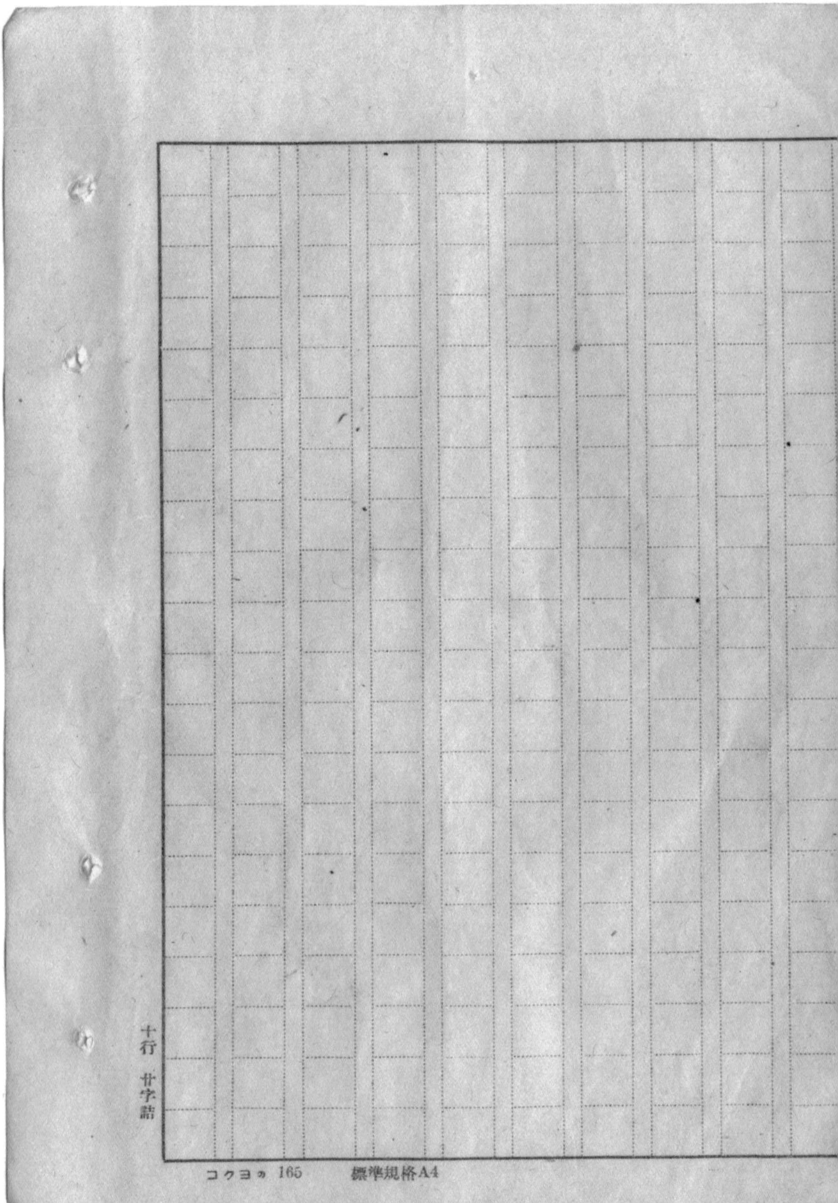
十行　廿字詰
コクヨ の 165　標準規格A4

太初의 아츰

봄날 아츰도 아니고
여름, 가을, 겨울,
그런날 아츰도 아닌 아츰에

빨ㅣ간 꽃이 피여낫네,
해ㅅ빛이 푸른데,

그 前날밤

그 前날 밤에

모든 것이 마련되엿네

사랑은 뱀과 함께

毒은 어린 꽃과 함께

No.

또 太初의 아침

하얗게 눈이 덮이엿고
電信柱가 잉잉 울어
하나님 말슴이 들려온다.

무슨 啓示일가.

발리

봄이 오면
罪를 짓고
눈이
밝어

이브가 解産하는 수고를 다하면

無花果 잎사귀로 부끄런데를 가리고

나는 이마에 땀을 흘려야겠다.

1941. 5. 31.

十行 廿字詰

コクヨ ロ 165 標準規格A4

No.

새벽이 올때까지

다들 죽어가는 사람들에게
검은 옷을 입히시오.

다들 살어가는 사람들에게
흰 옷을 입히시오.

그리고 한 寢臺에

~~[illegible]~~ 잠을 재우시오

다들 울거들랑

젖을 먹이시오

이제 — 새벽이 오면

나팔소리 들려 올게외다.

一九四一.

No.

0. 무서운時間

거 나를 부르는것이 누구요,

가랑닢 입파리 푸르러 나오는 그늘인데,

나 아직 여기 呼吸이 남어 있소.

한번도 손들어 보지못한 나를

손들어 표할 하늘도 없는 나를

35

어디에 내 한몸둘 하늘이 있어
나를 부르는 것이오.

일이 마치고 내 죽는날 아츰에는
서럽지도 않은 가랑닢이 떨어질텐데……

나를 부르지마오.

一九四一. 二. 七

No.

十字架

쫓아오든 햇빛인데
지금 教會堂 꼭대기
十字架에 걸리였습니다.

尖塔이 저렇게도 높은데
어떻게 올라갈수 있을가요.

휘파람이나 불며
서성거리다가,

괴로왔든 사나이,
幸福한 예수·그리스도에게
처럼
十字架가 許諾된다면

목아지를 드리우고
꽃처럼 피여나는 피를

어두어가는 하늘밑에
조용히 흘리겠읍니다.

一九四一、五、三一、

38

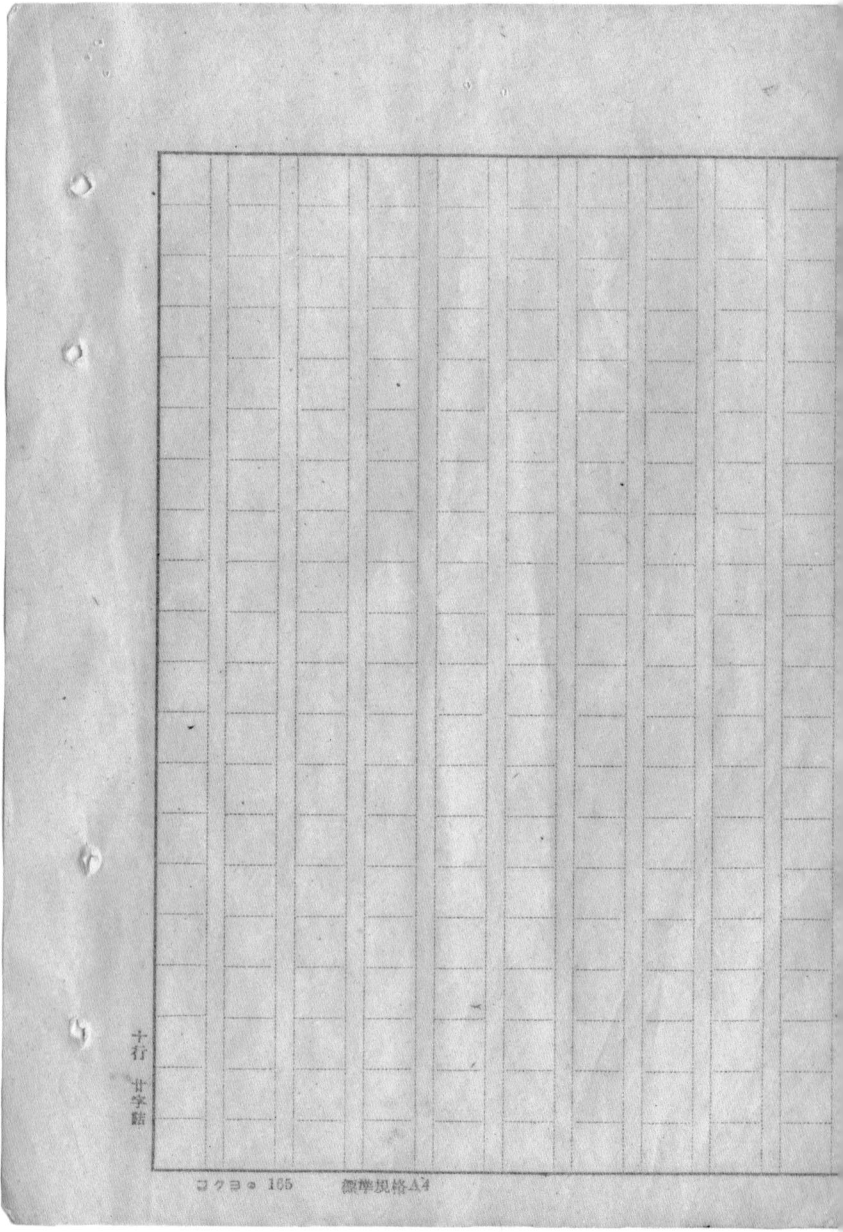
十行 廿字詰
コクヨ ○ 165
標準規格A4

바람이 불어

바람이 어디로부터 불어와
어디로 불려가는 것일가、

바람이 부는데
내 괴로움에는 理由가 없다。

내 괴로움에는 理由가 없을가、

41

단 한 女子를 사랑한 일도 없다。
時代를 슬퍼한 일도 없다。

바람이 작고 부는데
내 발이 반석우에 섯다。

강물이 작고 흐르는데
내발이 언덕우에 섯다。

一九四一. 六. 二

No.

슬픈 族屬

흰 수건이 검은 머리를 두르고
흰 고무신이 거츤발에 걸리우다.

흰 저고리 치마가 슬픈 몸집을 가리고
흰 띠가 가는 허리를 질끈 동이다.

一九三八、九、

43

十行 廿字詰

コクヨ ◎ 165　標準規格A4

No.

눈감고 간다

太陽을 사모하는 아이들아

별을 사랑하는 아이들아

밤이 어두었는데

눈감고 가거라.

가진바, 씨앗을

44

뿌리면서 가거라

발뿌리에 돌이 채이거든

감었든 눈을 왓작떠라.

一九四一、五、三一、

No.

또다른 故鄕

故鄕에 돌아온날 밤에

내 白骨이 따라와 한방에 누었다.

어둔 房은 宇宙로 通하고

하늘에선가 소리처럼 바람이 불어온다.

어둠속에 곱게 風化作用하는

白骨을 드려다 보며
눈물 짓는것이 내가 우는 것이냐
白骨이 우는 것이냐
아름다운 魂이 우는 것이냐

志操 높은 개는
밤을 새워 어둠을 짖는다.

어둠을 짖는 개는
나를 쫓는 것일게다.

十行 廿字詰

コクヨ 165 標準規格A4

No.

가자 가자
쫓기우는 사람처럼 가자
白骨몰래
아름다운 또 다른 故鄕에 가자.

一九四一、九

十行 廿字詰

コクヨの 165　標準規格A4

No.

길

잃어 버렸습니다.
무얼 어디다 잃었는지 몰라
두손이 주머니를 더듬어
길에 나아갑니다.

돌과 돌과 돌이 끝없이 연달어
길은 돌담을 끼고 갑니다.

51

담은 쇠문을 굳게 닫어
길우에 긴 그림자를 드리우고

길은 아츰에서 저녁으로
저녁에서 아츰으로 통했습니다.

돌담을 더듬어 눈물 짓다
처다보면 하늘은 부끄럽게 푸릅니다.

十行 廿字詰

No.

풀 한포기 없는 이 길을 걷는 것은
담 저쪽에 내가 남어 있는 까닭이고,

내가 사는 것은, 다만,
잃은 것을 찾는 까닭입니다.

一九四一, 九, 三一,

53

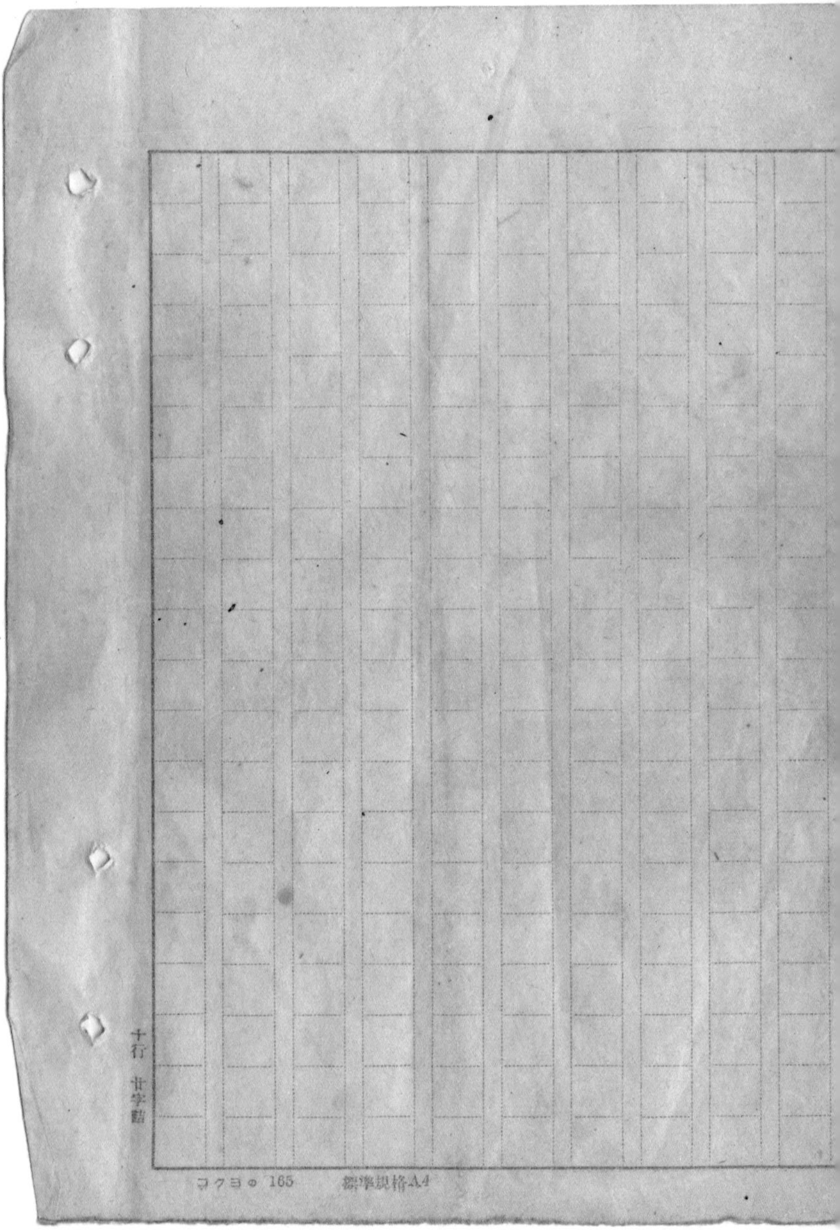

No.

별헤는 밤

季節이 지나가는 하늘에는
가을로 가득 차 있습니다.

나는 아무 걱정도 없이
가을속의 별들을 다 헤일듯합니다.

가슴속에 하나 둘 새겨지는 별을

이제 다 못헤는 것은
쉬이 아츰이 오는 까닭이오
來日밤이 남은 까닭이오,
아직 나의 靑春이 다하지 않은 까닭입
니다.

별하나에 追憶과
별하나에 사랑과
별하나에 쓸쓸함과
별하나에 憧憬과

No.

별하나에 詩와

별하나에 어머니, 어머니,

어머님, 나는 별하나에 아름다운 말

한마디식 불러봅니다. 小學校때 冊床을

같이 했든 아이들의 일홈과 佩, 鏡, 玉

이런 異國少女들의 일홈과 벌서 애기

어머니 된 게집애들의 일홈과, 가난한

이웃사람들의 일홈과, 비둘기, 강아지, 토

끼, 노새, 노루, 「프랑시쓰·짬」「라이넬·마

리아·릴케 이런 詩人의 일홈을 불러봅니다.

이네들은 너무나 멀리 있습니다.
별이 아슬이 멀듯이,

어머님,
그리고 당신은 멀리 北間島에 계십니다.

나는 무엇인지 그리워

十行 廿字詰

コクヨの 165 標準規格A4

No.

이 많은 별빛이 나린 언덕우에
내 일홈자를 써보고,
흙으로 덮허 버리엿습니다.

딴은 밤을 새워 우는 버레는
부끄러운 일홈을 슬퍼하는 까닭입니다.

(一九四一, 十一, 五.)

그러나 겨울이 지나고 나의 별에도 봄이 오면
무덤우에 파란 잔디가 피여나듯이
내 일홈자 묻힌 언덕우에도

十行 廿字詰
165
標準規格A4

달을 쏘다

번거롭던 四圍가 잠잠해지고 時計소리
가 또렷하나 보니 밤은 저윽히 깊을대
로 깊은 모양이다. 보든 冊子를 冊床머리
에 미러놓고 잠자리를 수습한다음 잠옷
을 걸치는 것이다. '딱' 스윗치소리와 함께
電燈을 끄고 窓역의 寢臺에 드러누으니
이때가지 밝은 휘양찬 달밤이었든 것을

感覺치 못하였댔다。 이것도 밝은 電燈의
惠澤이었을가。
나의 陋醜한 房이 달빛에 잠겨 아름
다운 그림이 된다는 것보담도 오히려 슬
픈 船艙이 되는 것이다。 창살이 이마로
부터 코마루、 입술 이렇게 하야 가슴에
여맨 손등에 까지 어른거려 나의 마음을
간지리는 것이다。 옆에 누운 분의 숨소리에
房은 무시무시해 진다。 아이처럼 황황해
지는 가슴에 눈을 · 치떠서 밖을 내다보니

十行 廿字詰

コクヨ● 165

가을하늘은 역시 맑고 우거진 松林은
한폭의 墨畵다. 날빼춘 솔가지에 꼴가지
미 산다저 빠람인양 솨ㅡ소리가 날듯하
다. 들리는 것은 啄木소리와 숨소리와 귀
또리울음뿐 썩적고던 寒窓舍도 절깐보다
더한층 고요한 것이 아니냐?
나는 같은 思念에 잠기우기 한창이다.
또는 사랑스런 아가씨를 私有할수 있는
아름다운 想華도 좋고, 어린적 未練을
두고온 故鄕의 鄕愁도 좋거니와 그보

답 손쉽게 表現못할 深刻한 그무엇이 있다.

바다를 건너온 H君의 편지사연을 곰곰생각할수록 사람과사람사이의 感情이란 微妙한것이다。 感傷的인 그에게도 必然코 가을은 왔나부다。

편지는 너무나 지나치지 않었든가 그中한토막,

H君아! 나는 지금 울며울며 이글을 쓴다。 이밤도 달이 뜨고、 바람이 불고、

人間인께다리에 가을이란 흙냄새도 · 안다。

情의 눈물 따뜻한 藝術學徒였던 情의 눈물도 이밤이 마지막이다。

또 마지막 편으로 이런 句節이 있다。

당신은 나를 永遠히 쪼차버리는 것이고 直할것이오。

나는 이 글의 뉴안스를 解得할수있다。

그러나 事實나는 그에게 애돈 소리한마디 한일이 없고 설흔글 한쪽 보낸일이 없지 아니한가, 생각건대 이 罪는 다만 가을에

64

게 지워 보낼수빡게 없다.
紅顔書法으로 이런 斷案을 나리는 것
은 외람한 일이나 동무란 한낫 괴로운
存在요 友情이란 진정코 위트렵은 잔이
떠노흔 물이다. 이말을 反對할者 누구랴.
그러나 知己하나 엇기 힘든다하거늘 알
뜰한 동무하나 일허버린다는것이 살을배
여내는 아픔이다.
나는 나를 庭園에서 發見하고 窓을
넘어 나왓다든가 房門을 열고 나왓다든

가 웨 나왓느냐하는 어리석은 생각에 頭腦를 괴롭게할 必要는 없는것이야. 다만 귀뚜람이 울음에도 수집어지는 코쓰모쓰 앞에 그윽히서서 딱터빨링쓰의 銅像 그림자처럼 슬퍼지면 그만이다. 나는 이마음을 아무에게나 轉嫁식힐 심보는 없다. 옷깃은 敏感이여서 달빛에도 싸늘히 추어지고 가을 이슬이란 선득선득하여서 설은 사나이의 눈물인 것이다.

발거름은 몸둥이를 옮겨 못가게 귀찮

줄때 못속에도 역시 가을이 있고, 三更이 있고, 나무가 있고, 달이 있다.

그 刹那 가을이 怨望스럽고 달이 미워진다. 더듬어 돌을 찾어 달을 向하야 죽어라고 팔매질을 하엿다. 痛快! 달은 散散히 부서지고 말엇다. 그러나 놀랏든 물결이 자저들때 오래잖허 달은 도로 살아난것이 아니냐, 문득 하늘을 처다보니 얄미운 달은 머리우에서 빈정대는 것을 .——

67

나는 곳곳한 나무가를 고나 떼를 재서 줄을 메워 훌륭한 활을 만들엇다。그리고 좀 단단한 갈대로 활살을 삼아 武士의 마음을 먹고 달을 쏘다。

—끝—

「一九三八 十月 脫稿。
一九三九 一月 朝鮮日報
學生欄 發表」

十行　廿字詰

コクヨ◎　165

별똥떨어진데

밤이다.

하늘은 푸르다 못해 濃灰色으로 캄캄하나 별들만은 또렷또렷 빛난다. 침침한 어둠뿐만 아니라 오삭오삭 춥다. 이 육중한 氣流가운데 自嘲하는 한 젊은 이가 있다. 그를 나라고 불러두자.

나는 이 어둠에서 胚胎되고 이 어둠

에서 生長하여서 아직도 이 어둠속에 그대로 生存하나 보다. 이제 내가 갈곳이 어딘지 몰라 허우적거리는 것이다. 하기는 나는 世紀의 焦点인듯 憔悴하다. 별뜻 생각키기에는 내바닥을 받듯이 받들어주는 것도 없고 그렇다고 내머리를 갑빡이 나려누르는 아모것도 없는듯하다 만은 內幕은 그리치도 않다. 나는 도무 自由스럽지 못하다. 다만 나는 없는듯 있는 하로사리처럼 虛空에

浮遊하는 한꽃에 지나지 않는다. 이것이 하로사리처럼 輕快하다면 마침 多幸할 것인데 그렇지를 못하구나!

이 꽃의 對稱位置에 또하나 다른 밝음(明)의 焦꽃이 도사리고 있는듯 생각키다. 덥석 웅키였으면 잡힐듯도 하다. 만은 그것을 휘잡기에는 나自身이 鈍質이라는 것보다 오히려 내마음에 아무런 準備도 배포치 못한것이 아니냐.

러 들이기에도 또다른 한가닥 구실을 치르지 않으면 안될가 보다.

이밤이 나에게있어 버린적처럼 하낱 恐怖의 장막인 것은 벌서 흘러간 傳說이오. 따라서 이밤이 享樂의 도가니라는 이야기도 나의 念頭에선 아직 清化식히지 못할 돌덩이다. 오로지 밤은 나의 挑戰의 好敵이면 그만이다.

이것이 생생한 觀念世界에만 머므른다-면 애석한 일이다. 어둠속에 깜박깜박

조을며 다닥다닥 나란니 한 草家들이 아름다운 詩의 華詞가 될 수 있다는 것은 벌서 지나간 쩨네레슌의 이야기요, 오늘에 있어서는 다만 말못하는 悲劇의 背景이다.

이제 닭이 홰를 치면서 맵짠 울음을 뽑아 밤을 쫓고 어둠을 즞내몰아 동켠으로 휘―ㄴ이 새벽이란 새로운 손님을 불러온다 하자. 하나 輕妄스럽게 그리 반가워 할 것은 없다.

이 있다하더래도 이 마을은 그대로 暗澹하고 나도 그대로 暗澹하고 対하여서 너나 나나 이 가랑지길에서 躊躇躊躇 아니치 못할 存在들이 아니냐.

나무가 있다.

그는 나의 오란 리웃이오, 벗이다. 그런고 그와 내가 性格이나 環境이나 生活이 共通한데 있어서가 아니다. 말하자면 極端과 極端사이에도 愛情이 貫通할 수 있다는 奇蹟的인 交合의 한標本에 지

十行 廿字詰

コクヨ 165

나지 못할것이다。

나는 처음 그를 퍽 不幸한 存在로 가소롭게 여겼다。 그의 앞에 설때 슬퍼지고 惻隱한 마음이 앞을 가리곤 하였다。 만은 오늘 돌이켜 생각건대 나무처럼 幸福한 生物은 다시 없을듯 하다。 굳음에는 이루 비길데 없는 바위에도 그리 탐탁치는 못할망정 滋養分이 있다 하거늘 어디로 간들 生의 뿌리를 박지

을 소나, 칙칙하면 솔솔 솔바람이 불어
오고, 심심하면 새가 와서 노래를 부르
다 가고, 졸졸하면 한줄기 비가 오고,
밤이면 數많은 별들과 오손도손 이야기
할수있고 —— 보다 나무는 行動의 方向이
란 거치장스런 課題에 逢着하지 않고
人為的으로든 偶然으로서든 誕生식혀준
자리를 직혀 無盡無窮한 營養素를 吸取
하고 玲瓏한 해ㅅ빛을 빨아드려 손쉽게
生活을 營為하고 오로지 하늘만 빠라고

뻐더질수 있는것이 무엇보다 幸福스럽지
않으냐.
이 밤도 課題를 풀지 못하야 안타까운
나의 마음에 나무의 마음이 漸漸 올마오
는듯하고, 行動할수 있는 자랑을 자랑치
못함에 뼈저리는듯 하나 나의 젊은 先
輩의 雄辯이 曰 先輩도 믿지 못할것이라
니 그러면 怜悧한 나무에게 나의 方向
을 물어야 할것인가.
어디로 가야 하느냐 東이 어디냐 西

가 어디냐 南이 어디냐 北이 어디냐

아라! 저별이 번쩍 흐른다。 별똥 떨어진

데가 내가 갈곳인가 보다。 하면 별똥아

! 꼭 떨어져야 할곳에 떨어져야 한다。

十行 廿字詰

花園에 꽃이 핀다

개나리, 진달래, 앉은뱅이, 라일락,
문들레, 찔레, 복사, 들장미, 해당화, 모란,
릴리, 창포, 추립, 카네슌, 봉선화, 백일홍,
채송화, 따리아, 해바라기, 코스모스 ──
코스모스가 홀홀히 떨어지는 날 宇宙의 마
지막은 아닙니다. 여기에 푸른 하늘이 높아
지고, 빨간 노란 단풍이 꽃에 못지 아니

게 가지마다 물들었다가 귀또리 울음이 끊어짐과 함께 단풍의 세계가 문허지고, 그우에 하로밤 사이에 소복이 흰 눈이 나려, 나려 쌓이고 火爐에는 빨간 숯불이 피여오르고 많은 이야기와 많은 일이 이 火爐가에서 일우어집니다.

讀者諸賢! 여러분은 이 글이 씌워지는 때를 獨特한 季節로 짐작해서는 아니됩니다. 봄, 여름, 가을, 겨울, 어느 철로나 想定하셔도 無妨합니다. 사실 一年

TS NO. 5 10 × 20

내내 봄일수는 없읍니다. 하나 이花園에
는 사철내 봄이 靑春들과 함께 싱싱하게 등대하여 있다
고 하면 過分한 自己宣傳일가요. 하나의 꽃밭이 이루어지도록 손쉽게 되는 것이 아니라 고생과 노력이 있어야 하는 것입니다.
딴은 얼마의 單語를 모아 이 拙文을 지적거리는데도 내머리는 그
렇게 明晳한 것은 못됩니다. 한해동안을 내
頭腦로써가 아니라 몸으로써 일일이 헤아려
細胞사이마다 간직해 두어서야 겨우 몇줄의 글이 이루어집니다. 그리하여 나에게 있어
봄바람의 苦悶에 짜들고, 綠陰의 倦怠에 쓰들고,
가을 하늘 感傷에 울고, 爐邊의 思索에 졸다가
이 몇줄의 글과 함께 나의

꽃밭이 이루도록 숙고(熟考)한 고생이있다。
温情의 거리에서 원수를 만나며 속옥을 본집

一命은 이루어집니다.
시간을 먹는 (따분한 時間) 하이 말의 無味는 칠판
발을 때에서 보신 분화 없어 보신 분은 누구나
아실 것입니다. 그것은 確實히 즐거운 일임
에 틀림없읍니다。 休講한다는 것보
다. 못 한 시간 宿題를 못해왔다든가.
또 분하고 졸리고 한 때. 한 시간의 休講은 전 실로
살로 가는 것이 에서, 萬一 教授가 不便하
새에서 못 오셨다고 하더라도 허우리들의
禮儀를 가출시 가 없는 것입니다.

TS NO. 5 10 × 20

83

그러나 이것을 ... 라고 ... 하셔서 아
니 됩니다. 여기에 花園이 있습니다.
한포기 꽃과 함께 웃을 수 있습니다. 노—
트장을 적시는 것보다 中... 標에 무처
글줄과 씨름하는 것보다 더 ... 眞理를
探求할 수 있는지 보다 더 많은 知識을 獲得
할 수 있을런지 보다 더 効果的인 成果가 있을
지를 누가 言語하겠습니까.
나는 이 貴한 時間을 슬그머니 동무들
을 떠나서 단 혼자 花園에 거닐 수 있습니

85

다. 단 혼자 꽃들과 풀들과 이야기 할수 있었다는 것이 얼마나 幸福한 일이 겠습니까, 침묵 하는 溫情으로 이들을 대할수 있고 그들은 우슴으로 나를 맞어 줍니다. 그 우슴을 눈물로 答한다는 것은 나의 感傷일가요, 孤獨, 靜寂도 寂寞히 아름다운 것임에 틀림이 없으나. 여기에 또 새로마음을 주는 동무가 없는 것도 多幸한 일이 아닐수 없습니다. 우리 花園속에 보인, 동무들 중에, 집에 學費를 請求하는

될지를 쓰는 날저녁이면 생각하였고 생각하다든 줄 깨우 몇줄 써본다는 A君, 깁버해야할 書留(通綠用紙封套)를 받어든 손이 떨린다는 B君, 사랑을 爲해 애서는 밥맛을 잃고 잠을 이저버린다는 C君, 思想的 撞着에 自殺을 期約한다는 D君, ―!―.

나는 이 여러동무들의 가륵한 心情을 내것인것처럼 理解할수 있습니다. 서로 너그러운 마음으로 대할수 있습니다.

나는 世界觀, 人生觀, 이런 좀더 큰 問

흐리운다.

題보다 바람과 구름과 햇빛과 나무와 友情, 이런 것들에 더 많이 괴로워해 왔는지도 모르겠습니다. 단지 이 말이 나의 遠이다. 나는 自身을 그리우는데 지나날을 뿐일까요. 一生, 一般은 現代 學生道德이 腐敗했다고 말합니다. 스승을 섬길 줄을 모른다고들 합니다. 옳은 말씀들입니다. 부조러울 때로는 읽니다. 하나 이 절함을 괴로워하는 우리들 억깨에 지워 짐을 내쫓아 버려야 하는 것을, 우리들의 아픈데를 알어주는 스승.

TS NO. 5 10 × 20

우리들의 생채기를 어루만저주는 따뜻한 世界가 있다면 빛을 발한 道德일지언정 기우려 스승을 眞心으로 尊敬하겠습니다. 溫情의 거리에서 원수를 맺는다면 손목을 붙잡고 목노아 울겠습니다.

世上은 해를 거듭. 砲聲에 떠들석하것만 극히 조용한 가운데 우리들 동산에서 서로 融合할수 있고 理解할수 있고 從前의 가졌는 것은 勞動의. 運動結果일까요.

봄이가고, 여름이가고, 가을, 코스모스가

89

홀홀히 떠러지는 날 宇宙의 마치막은 아
닙니다. 단풍의 世界가 있고, ―履霜而堅氷
至― 서리를 밟거든 어름이 굳어질 것을
각오하라, 가 아니라, 우리는 서릿발에 끼
친 落葉을 밟으면서 멀리 봄이 올 것을
믿습니다.
爐邊에서 많은 일이, 일우어질 것입니다.